THE BEST NBA
CENTERS
OF ALL TIME

By Patrick Donnelly

www.abdopublishing.com

Published by Abdo Publishing, a division of ABDO, PO Box 398166, Minneapolis, Minnesota 55439. Copyright © 2015 by Abdo Consulting Group, Inc. International copyrights reserved in all countries. No part of this book may be reproduced in any form without written permission from the publisher. SportsZone™ is a trademark and logo of Abdo Publishing.

Printed in the United States of America, North Mankato, Minnesota
032014
092014

Cover Photos: AP Images (left); Chris Urso/AP Images (right)
Interior Photos: AP Images, 1 (left), 7, 13, 15, 19, 21, 23, 25, 31, 35, 41; Chris Urso/AP Images, 1 (right); Ed Maloney/AP Images, 9; Gene Herrick/AP Images, 11; David F. Smith/AP Images, 17; Carlos Rene Perez/AP Images, 27; Joe Giza/AP Images, 29; Bob Galbraith/AP Images, 33; R. Saxon/AP Images, 37; George Widman/AP Images, 39; Peter A. Southwick/AP Images, 43; Andrew Innerarity/AP Images, 45; David Zalubowski/AP Images, 47; Tim Sharp/AP Images, 49; Kevin Larkin/AP Images, 51; Ron Frehm/AP Images, 53; Scott Troyanos/AP Images, 55; David J. Phillip/AP Images, 57; Michael Conroy/AP Images, 59; Mark Terrill/AP Images, 61

Editor: Chrös McDougall
Series Designer: Christa Schneider

Library of Congress Control Number: 2014932917

Cataloging-in-Publication Data
Donnelly, Patrick.
 The best NBA centers of all time / Patrick Donnelly.
   p. cm. -- (NBA's best ever)
ISBN 978-1-62403-409-1
1. National Basketball Association--Juvenile literature.   2. Centers (Basketball)--Juvenile literature.   I. Title.
796.323--dc23

                                        2014932917

TABLE OF CONTENTS

INTRODUCTION

Basketball fans have long been fascinated by centers.

The National Basketball Association's (NBA's) best centers earn their place in history with hard work and impressive skills. But they truly stand out because of their size. It is unusual to see a man standing 7 feet tall. It is even more unusual to see him run, jump, shoot, and pass with the best athletes in the world. Many of the best centers have had giant personalities to match their massive bodies. But they are best remembered for their unique ability to play the game above the rim.

Here are some of the best centers in NBA history.

GEORGE MIKAN

Basketball was not yet a major sport in the 1940s. George Mikan helped change that in a hurry.

Mikan was the NBA's first true "big man." He also was the game's first true superstar. Mikan's legend grew during his college career at DePaul University in Chicago. Word spread of the giant who could swat away a ball from above the rim. That was hard to imagine in a day when the game's best players were short and quick.

Mikan joined the Minneapolis Lakers in 1947. That was two years before the Lakers joined the NBA. He already was a household name. The Lakers visited New York to play the Knicks in December 1949. The marquee outside Madison Square Garden that night showed how famous Mikan had become. The sign simply read: "Geo. Mikan vs. Knicks."

Minneapolis Lakers center George Mikan tips in a basket while being fouled during a 1949 game against the New York Knicks.

With his thick glasses and No. 99 jersey, Mikan stood out on the court. He was strong but also had a soft shooting touch. He mastered a hook shot with either hand. And the shot was impossible to defend. He also ran the court well for a big man.

The combination of those skills helped Mikan lead the NBA in scoring three times. He also led the Lakers to six championships in seven seasons. Four of those titles came after the Lakers joined the NBA.

In some ways, every center who followed owes his career, in part, to Mikan. Players today still practice the "Mikan Drill." It helps them perfect rebounding and shooting with both hands.

19–18

The score when the Fort Wayne Pistons beat the Lakers in 1950. The Pistons held the ball for long periods of time to keep it away from George Mikan. That game led to the NBA's adoption of a 24-second shot clock in 1954.

NBA star center Shaquille O'Neal showed just how much Mikan meant to the game. When Mikan died in 2005, O'Neal paid for the funeral.

"Without No. 99, there is no me," O'Neal said.

The Minneapolis Lakers' George Mikan goes for a shot against a college All-Star team in 1949.

GEORGE MIKAN

Hometown: Joliet, Illinois

College: DePaul University

Height, Weight: 6 feet 10, 245 pounds

Birth Date: June 18, 1924

Team: Minneapolis Lakers (1948–54, 1955–56)

All-Star Games: 4 (1951–54)

First-Team All-NBA: 1949–50, 1950–51, 1951–52, 1952–53, 1953–54

BILL RUSSELL

Bill Russell was a big winner in his career. That showed in 1956 and 1957. It began in the spring of 1956. Russell led the University of San Francisco to its second straight collegiate national title. That summer, Russell captained Team USA to an Olympic gold medal in Melbourne, Australia. The following spring, the rookie led the NBA in rebounding average. And he capped off the season by leading the Boston Celtics to the league title.

No other player has ever won collegiate, Olympic, and NBA titles in consecutive years. It is not surprising that Russell was the man to do it, though. After all, his Celtics teams won the NBA championship 11 times in his 13 seasons in Boston. That is more titles than any other player has won in NBA history through 2013.

Boston Celtics center Bill Russell attempts a shot against the Minneapolis Lakers in 1957.

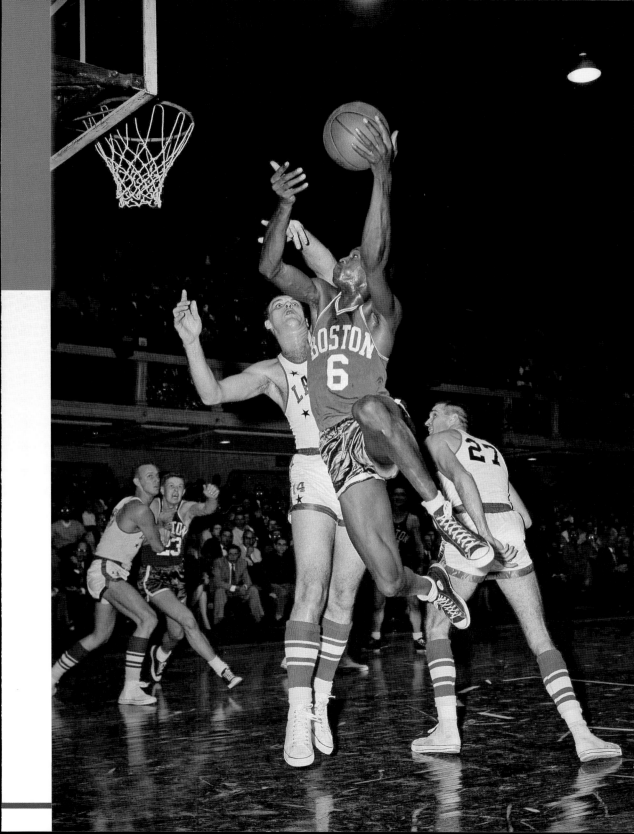

Russell won two of those titles as a player/coach. He also was the first black coach in NBA history.

Russell was not a skilled player at first. But his college coach saw potential in his long limbs and big hands. Through hard work, Russell saw he could change a game with his defense. He could keep an opposing center under wraps. Plus, he could use his speed and quickness to help teammates guard their men.

Russell carried those skills over to his NBA career. He dominated games from under the basket. The league did not keep track of blocked shots in those days. But if it had, Russell surely would have led the NBA most years. His steady defense and leadership made him the key to Boston's great teams in the 1960s.

5

The number of NBA Most Valuable Player (MVP) Awards Bill Russell won. Through 2013, only one player had won more.

The Celtics' Bill Russell rises above a St. Louis Hawks defender to attempt a shot during a 1957 game.

BILL RUSSELL

Hometown: Monroe, Louisiana
College: University of San Francisco
Height, Weight: 6 feet 10, 215 pounds
Birth Date: February 12, 1934
Team: Boston Celtics (1956–69)
All-Star Games: 12 (1958–69)
MVP Awards: 1957–58, 1960–61, 1961–62, 1962–63, 1964–65
First-Team All-NBA: 1958–59, 1962–63, 1964–65
All-Defensive Team: 1968–69

WILT CHAMBERLAIN

Wilt Chamberlain was taller and stronger than most players of his era. The man known as "The Big Dipper" already held the NBA record for points in a game with 78. But one night in 1962, he put that record far out of reach.

His Philadelphia Warriors were beating the New York Knicks. Chamberlain had 41 points at halftime. He was up to 69 by the end of the third quarter. But Chamberlain wanted to do more than simply break his record. He wanted to reach a number everyone would remember.

He did so with 46 seconds left in the game. The 7-foot-1 superstar dunked the ball. That gave him an even 100 points. The Warriors' radio announcer could not hide his excitement: "He made it! A Dipper dunk! The most amazing scoring performance of all time! One hundred points for the Big Dipper!"

Philadelphia Warriors center Wilt Chamberlain puts up a shot against the Boston Celtics during a 1962 game.

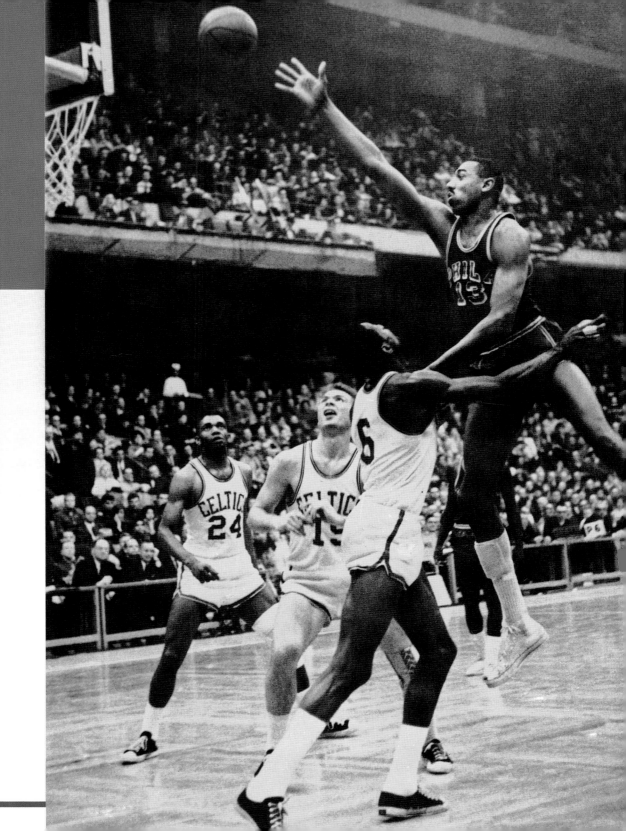

Others have tried to match the feat.

Yet through 2013, no player had scored more than 81 points in a single game.

Chamberlain went down as one of the NBA's all-time best players. He retired with more points and rebounds than any other player. He also was the reason behind many new rules. For example, Chamberlain was so tall he could supposedly leap and dunk the ball when shooting free throws. So that was outlawed. Chamberlain was dominant rebounding under the basket as well. So the NBA responded by widening the lane. That helped give other players a chance.

Chamberlain had a diverse background. He played at times with the Harlem Globetrotters.

23,924

The number of rebounds Wilt Chamberlain had in his career. That was the most of any player in NBA history through 2013.

After he retired from basketball, he became a professional volleyball player. He also acted in movies and ran marathons. Chamberlain made sure he would be remembered for more than just scoring 100 points in a game.

Los Angeles Lakers center Wilt Chamberlain looks to pass during a 1972 playoff game against the New York Knicks.

WILT CHAMBERLAIN

Hometown: Philadelphia, Pennsylvania

College: University of Kansas

Height, Weight: 7 feet 1, 275 pounds

Birth Date: August 21, 1936

Teams: Philadelphia/San Francisco Warriors (1959–65)
Philadelphia 76ers (1965–68)
Los Angeles Lakers (1968–73)

All-Star Games: 13 (1960–69, 1971–73)

MVP Awards: 1959–60, 1965–66, 1966–67, 1967–68

First-Team All-NBA: 1959–60, 1960–61, 1961–62, 1963–64,
1965–66, 1966–67, 1967–68

All-Defensive Team: 1971–72, 1972–73

NATE THURMOND

Many basketball fans love statistics.

One statistical feat is called the triple-double. That is when a player has double figures—at least 10—in three different stat categories in one game. Nate Thurmond went one step further. On October 18, 1974, he recorded the first official quadruple-double in NBA history. Thurmond had 22 points, 14 rebounds, 13 assists, and 12 blocked shots in a game.

The NBA did not start officially tracking blocked shots and steals until 1973–74. That means the feat could have happened before. But through 2013, only three players had done it since Thurmond.

Thurmond began his NBA career in a good spot. He played alongside the great Wilt Chamberlain with the San Francisco Warriors. Thurmond quickly showed he could hold his own against the NBA's other great centers.

San Francisco Warriors center Nate Thurmond posts up against Milwaukee Bucks center Lew Alcindor in 1971.

The Warriors traded Chamberlain the next season. And for the next 10 years, Thurmond was the anchor for some great teams in San Francisco.

Thurmond was then traded to the Chicago Bulls. He posted his quadruple-double in his first game in Chicago. The Bulls made the playoffs that season. However, they traded Thurmond to the Cleveland Cavaliers the next year. Out of nowhere, the Cavaliers made a run to the conference finals. Thurmond got much of the credit for their improvement.

Thurmond was a great rebounder and a tough defender. He always made players work hard for their points.

"When I score on Nate, I know I've done something," Kareem Abdul-Jabbar once said. "He sweats, and he wants you to sweat, too."

18

The number of rebounds Nate Thurmond had in one quarter on February 28, 1965. That was the most by any player in one quarter in NBA history through 2013.

The San Francisco Warriors' Nate Thurmond, *right*, battles for a rebound against the St. Louis Hawks in 1967.

NATE THURMOND

Hometown: Akron, Ohio

College: Bowling Green State University

Height, Weight: 6 feet 11, 225 pounds

Birth Date: July 25, 1941

Teams: San Francisco/Golden State Warriors (1963–74)
Chicago Bulls (1974–75)
Cleveland Cavaliers (1975–77)

All-Star Games: 7 (1965–68, 1970, 1973–74)

All-Defensive Team: 1968–69, 1970–71

WILLIS REED

The New York Knicks were in trouble.
Game 7 of the 1970 NBA Finals was about to begin. But New York's best player was not on the court.

Willis Reed was the Knicks' captain and star center. He had won the NBA's MVP Award that year. And in the first four games of the Finals, Reed had dominated the Los Angeles Lakers. He averaged almost 32 points per game. Even the great Wilt Chamberlain could not stop him.

But Reed had suffered a leg injury in Game 5. He could not play in Game 6. And the Lakers won that one easily. Without their captain, the Knicks would likely not stand a chance in Game 7.

The New York Knicks' Willis Reed rises up for a shot during the final seconds of a 1969 game against the Cincinnati Royals.

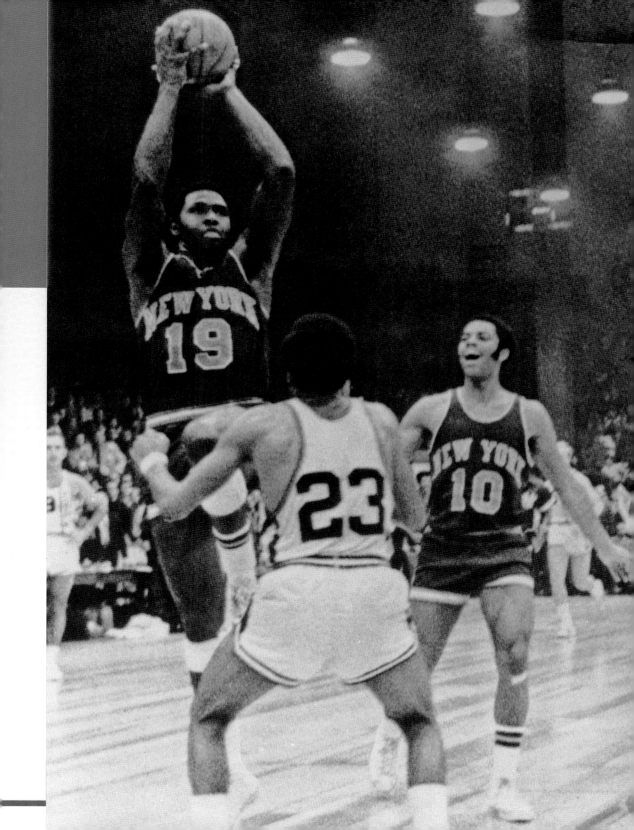

The opening tip neared. Still, no one knew whether Reed could play. Then, minutes before tip-off, Reed hobbled onto the court. He barely jumped at the opening tip. But Reed went on to score the Knicks' first two baskets. Those were the only points he scored that night. It did not matter. His teammates were inspired. They blew out the Lakers 113–99 to win their first NBA title.

That is the kind of leader Reed was. He was not the tallest or fastest player on the court. But he worked hard and played through pain. His left-handed jump shot was deadly from 15 feet (4.57 m). And he set brutal picks to free up his teammates.

The Knicks won another NBA title in 1973. And Reed was the Finals MVP in both of the Knicks' title runs. His No. 19 hangs above the court at Madison Square Garden, where fans still talk about his heroic night in 1970.

3

The number of MVP Awards Willis Reed earned in 1969–70. He was the All-Star Game MVP, the regular-season MVP, and the NBA Finals MVP.

Knicks center Willis Reed attempts a reverse layup against the Capital Bullets during a 1973 game.

WILLIS REED

Hometown: Hico, Louisiana
College: Grambling State University
Height, Weight: 6 feet 9, 235 pounds
Birth Date: June 25, 1942
Team: New York Knicks (1964–74)
All-Star Games: 7 (1965–71)
MVP Award: 1969–70
First-Team All-NBA: 1969–70
All-Defensive Team: 1969–70

WES UNSELD

Not all great centers need to be tall.
Wes Unseld proved that.

Unseld was listed at just 6 feet 7 inches. He later admitted he was probably an inch shorter than that. He often guarded players who were at least six inches taller than him. But by the end of the night, those players were usually left wondering how that "short guy" beat them.

Unseld did it by working hard. He also did a little bit of everything on the court. Some players are great scorers. Some have a knack for rebounding. Some are excellent passers. Some are tireless defenders. Unseld did all of those things well. If he had an off night in one part of his game, he could find other ways to help his team win.

Washington Bullets center Wes Unseld (41) battles for a rebound against the New York Knicks in a 1981 game.

Unseld was a star from the day he began his NBA career. He won the Rookie of the Year and MVP Award in his first season. Wilt Chamberlain was the only other player to do that through 2013. Unseld led the Baltimore/Capital/Washington Bullets to the playoffs in 12 straight seasons. They reached the NBA Finals four times in that span. His career highlight came in 1978. The Bullets won the team's first NBA title that year. Unseld was the Finals MVP.

Off the court, Unseld and his wife opened a private elementary school in Baltimore. He later worked in the Bullets' front office and was their head coach for parts of seven seasons.

23 years, 9 days

Wes Unseld's age when he won the 1968–69 MVP Award. He was the youngest NBA MVP until Derrick Rose won in 2011.

The Washington Bullets' Wes Unseld secures the ball after a rebound against the Houston Rockets in 1979.

WES UNSELD

Hometown: Louisville, Kentucky
College: University of Louisville
Height, Weight: 6 feet 7, 245 pounds
Birth Date: March 14, 1946
Team: Baltimore/Capital/Washington Bullets (1968–81)
All-Star Games: 5 (1969, 1971–73, 1975)
MVP Award: 1968–69
First-Team All-NBA: 1968–69

KAREEM
ABDUL-JABBAR

At age 38, Kareem Abdul-Jabbar heard the whispers. People thought he was washed up. His Los Angeles Lakers had reached the 1985 NBA Finals. But the rival Boston Celtics had thumped them in Game 1. Abdul-Jabbar had been badly outplayed by Boston center Robert Parish. The Lakers looked to be in trouble.

But Abdul-Jabbar would not go away that easily. During the next two days, he watched long hours of video. And he practiced until his coaches had to drag him off the court. In Game 2, he answered the whispers. Abdul-Jabbar scored 30 points and grabbed 17 rebounds. He even dished out eight assists and blocked three shots. More importantly, the Lakers won the game.

Kareem Abdul-Jabbar of the Los Angeles Lakers attempts a skyhook against the Boston Celtics during a 1986 game.

Los Angeles went on to win the series and the championship. Abdul-Jabbar was named the Finals MVP. He proved that he still had plenty of will to win.

The star center was born as Lew Alcindor. He changed his name in 1971 because he converted to Islam. Abdul-Jabbar won three national titles at the University of California, Los Angeles (UCLA). He was so hard to defend that dunking was outlawed in college basketball for almost 10 years.

But Abdul-Jabbar's game did not rely on just dunking. He could sink his famous skyhook with either hand. He also blocked at least 10 shots in a game seven times as a pro (blocks were not recorded until the 1973–74 season). He won six MVP Awards and six championships. When he retired from the NBA in 1989, he had scored more points and played more minutes than any player in league history. Those records still stood in 2013.

19

The number of All-Star Games for which Kareem Abdul-Jabbar was selected. That was still an NBA record through 2013.

The Lakers' Kareem Abdul-Jabbar posts up against a Detroit Pistons defender during a 1988 game.

KAREEM ABDUL-JABBAR

Hometown: New York, New York

College: UCLA

Height, Weight: 7 feet 2, 225 pounds

Birth Date: April 16, 1947

Teams: Milwaukee Bucks (1969–75)
Los Angeles Lakers (1975–89)

All-Star Games: 19 (1970–77, 1979–89)

MVP Awards: 1970–71, 1971–72, 1973–74, 1975–76, 1976–77, 1979–80

First-Team All-NBA: 1970–71, 1971–72, 1972–73, 1973–74, 1975–76, 1976–77, 1979–80, 1980–81, 1983–84, 1985–86

All-Defensive Team: 1973–74, 1974–75, 1978–79, 1979–80, 1980–81

ARTIS GILMORE

Artis Gilmore was a man of few words.
He played 18 professional seasons. During that time he was known as a quiet, almost shy person. But one night in 2011, he spoke a few words he had been waiting a long time to say.

"My name is Artis Gilmore, and I am a member of the Basketball Hall of Fame," he said during his acceptance speech.

Gilmore had come a long way. He grew up in northern Florida with nine brothers and sisters. And his family often was too poor to buy shoes for everyone. Still, young Gilmore grew to be one of the strongest players in NBA history.

In college, Gilmore led Jacksonville University to the national championship game. He also was one of only five players to average 20 points and 20 rebounds in his college career.

Artis Gilmore of the Kentucky Colonels, *top*, battles for a rebound against the Denver Nuggets in a 1976 game.

Gilmore then went on to the American Basketball Association (ABA). That league was a rival to the NBA. Gilmore was one of the ABA's biggest stars. He did not miss a game in five seasons with the Kentucky Colonels. He led the league in rebounding in four of those seasons. He also helped the Colonels win the 1975 ABA title.

The ABA merged with the NBA one year later. Some ABA teams disbanded. The players were made available to NBA teams in a draft. Gilmore was the first pick. The Chicago Bulls improved by 20 wins in their first season with Gilmore in the middle.

Gilmore was an ace shot-blocker and a strong rebounder. He led the NBA in field-goal percentage four years in a row. He also played in the All-Star Game five times in six years. And he wound up in the Basketball Hall of Fame.

.670

Artis Gilmore's field goal percentage in 1980–81. That was the fourth-highest percentage in NBA history through 2013.

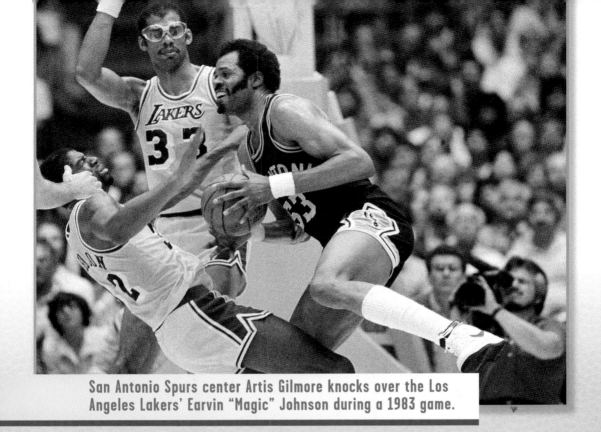

San Antonio Spurs center Artis Gilmore knocks over the Los Angeles Lakers' Earvin "Magic" Johnson during a 1983 game.

ARTIS GILMORE

Hometown: Chipley, Florida

College: Jacksonville University

Height, Weight: 7 feet 2, 240 pounds

Birth Date: September 21, 1949

Teams: Kentucky Colonels (1971–76)*;
Chicago Bulls (1976–82, 1987);
San Antonio Spurs (1982–87); Boston Celtics (1988)

All-Star Games: 11 (1972–76, 1978–79, 1981–83, 1986)*

MVP Award: 1971–72*

First-Team All-ABA: 1971–72, 1972–73, 1973–74, 1974–75,
1975–76

All-Defensive Team: 1972–73, 1973–74, 1974–75, 1975–76*

* Stats from 1976 and earlier are from the ABA

MOSES MALONE

Moses Malone kept it simple. The Philadelphia 76ers were heading into the 1983 playoffs. A reporter asked Malone how the 76ers would fare. The reply? "Fo', fo', fo'." Malone, in his strong Virginia accent, was saying the 76ers would sweep all three series in four games.

Malone's prediction missed by one game. The 76ers swept the New York Knicks in the first round. They then dropped one road game against the Milwaukee Bucks in the next round. A sweep of the Los Angeles Lakers in the NBA Finals capped the amazing run.

"Fo', fo', fo'" did not quite come true. But the players liked the phrase so much that their championship rings were engraved with "Fo', Five, Fo'."

The Philadelphia 76ers' Moses Malone, *top*, and the Los Angeles Lakers' Kareem Abdul-Jabbar battle for a rebound in 1983.

Malone was one of the first players to go straight from high school to the pros. He also became one of the greatest rebounders in league history. In his first 16 seasons, he averaged at least 10 rebounds 15 times. Malone was especially tough on the offensive end. The NBA started recording offensive rebounds in 1973–74. No player had recorded more of them through 2013.

All of those offensive rebounds led to a lot of layups and free throws. Malone scored at least 23.8 points per game eight times. He was seventh on the all-time points list through 2013.

Malone had already played eight pro seasons before being traded to the 76ers in 1982. Philadelphia fans saw him as the final piece of the puzzle. They were right. He teamed with the great Julius Erving to deliver the team's first title in 16 years. Even today, "Fo', fo', fo'" remains a rallying cry in Philadelphia.

5

The number of consecutive rebounding titles Moses Malone won from 1981 to 1985. He was the first player in NBA history to accomplish that feat.

Houston Rockets center Moses Malone goes up for an open shot against the Boston Celtics during a 1981 game.

MOSES MALONE

Hometown: Petersburg, Virginia

High School: Petersburg High School

Height, Weight: 6 feet 10, 215 pounds

Birth Date: March 23, 1955

Teams: Utah Stars (1974–75); Spirits of St. Louis (1975–76); Buffalo Braves (1976)*; Houston Rockets (1976–82); Philadelphia 76ers (1982–86, 1993–94); Washington Bullets (1986–88); Atlanta Hawks (1988–91); Milwaukee Bucks (1991–93); San Antonio Spurs (1994)

All-Star Games: 13 (1975, 1978–89)*

MVP Awards: 1978–79, 1981–82, 1982–83

First-Team All-NBA: 1978–79, 1981–82, 1982–83, 1984–85

All-Defensive Team: 1982–83

* Stats from 1976 and earlier are from the ABA

41

ROBERT PARISH

Thousands of players have appeared in NBA games. But no player has appeared in more of them than Robert Parish.

Parish played 21 seasons in the NBA. He took great care of his body. The 7-foot center relied on yoga, martial arts, bicycling, and weight training to stay fit during his career. He was still in great shape into his 40s. Parish played 74 games at age 42.

Parish grew up in Louisiana. He attended Centenary College in his hometown of Shreveport. He also was the captain of the US basketball team that won gold at the 1975 Pan American Games.

The following year, Parish entered the NBA with the Golden State Warriors. The Warriors had the NBA's best record in Parish's rookie season. Within four years, however, they were a losing team. In 1980, they traded Parish to the Boston Celtics.

Boston Celtics center Robert Parish rises for a shot against the Houston Rockets during the 1986 NBA Finals.

In Boston, Parish played with Hall of Fame forwards Larry Bird and Kevin McHale. The "Big Three" led the Celtics to three NBA titles in the 1980s.

Parish's teammates called him "Chief." Parish reminded them of a movie character with the same name. Both were strong and quiet. Parish used his strength and size to grab rebounds and block shots. But he was best known for his shooting touch. He made 53.7 percent of his shots during his career. Many of those came from outside of 10 feet (3.05 m). His trademark was a high-arcing shot that was hard to block.

"He's probably the best medium-range shooting big man in the history of the game," Hall of Fame center Bill Walton once said.

1,611

The number of NBA games Robert Parish played in his career. That was still an NBA record through 2013.

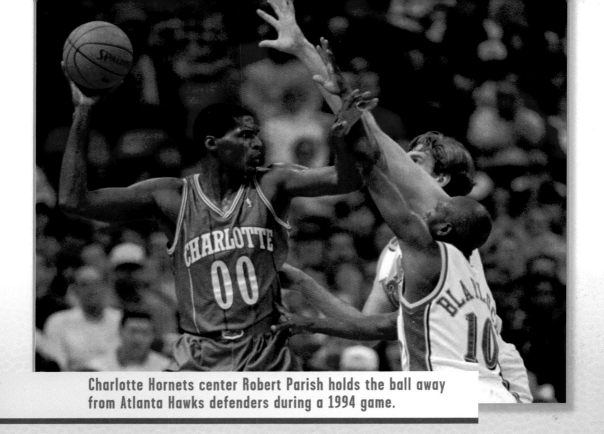

Charlotte Hornets center Robert Parish holds the ball away from Atlanta Hawks defenders during a 1994 game.

ROBERT PARISH

Hometown: Shreveport, Louisiana

College: Centenary College

Height, Weight: 7 feet, 230 pounds

Birth Date: August 30, 1953

Teams: Golden State Warriors (1976–80)
Boston Celtics (1980–94)
Charlotte Hornets (1994–96)
Chicago Bulls (1996–97)

All-Star Games: 9 (1981–87, 1990–91)

HAKEEM OLAJUWON

The 1984 NBA Draft was one of the most famous in history. Two teams that year passed on the legendary Michael Jordan. One of those teams picked a bust. The other picked Hakeem Olajuwon. According to Jordan, Olajuwon became the NBA's best center of all time.

"He is so versatile because of what he can give you from that position," Jordan said. "It's not just his scoring, not just his rebounding, or not just his blocked shots. People don't realize he was in the top seven in steals. He always made great decisions on the court. For all facets of the game, I have to give it to him."

Houston Rockets center Hakeem Olajuwon dunks the ball over a Denver Nuggets defender during a 2000 game.

That is high praise for a man who did not start playing basketball until age 15. Olajuwon grew up in Nigeria. His footwork and agility made him a natural soccer goalie growing up. But he left Nigeria to enroll at the University of Houston in 1980. His basketball skills were raw. However, the coaches saw he was a talented athlete. Olajuwon spent a summer playing against future Hall of Fame center Moses Malone. His game blossomed.

Olajuwon led Houston to two straight collegiate championship games. The hometown Houston Rockets then made him the first pick in the 1984 NBA Draft. Olajuwon went on to lead the Rockets to the NBA championship in 1994 and 1995. He was the MVP of the Finals both years.

Nicknamed "The Dream," Olajuwon was a master shot-blocker. He also led the league in rebounding twice and won two Defensive Player of the Year Awards.

3,830

The number of shots Hakeem Olajuwon blocked in his career. That was still an NBA record through 2013. The NBA began recording blocked shots in 1973–74.

The Rockets' Hakeem Olajuwon, *left*, and the New York Knicks' Patrick Ewing go for the tip to start a 1994 NBA Finals game.

HAKEEM OLAJUWON

Hometown: Lagos, Nigeria

College: University of Houston

Height, Weight: 7 feet, 255 pounds

Birth Date: January 21, 1963

Teams: Houston Rockets (1984–2001)
  Toronto Raptors (2001–02)

All-Star Games: 12 (1985–90, 1992–97)

MVP Award: 1993–94

First-Team All-NBA: 1986–87, 1987–88, 1988–89, 1992–93,
  1993–94, 1996–97

All-Defensive Team: 1986–87, 1987–88, 1989–90, 1992–93,
  1993–94

49

PATRICK EWING

It was the 1982 collegiate basketball championship game. A University of North Carolina player took his team's first shot. Georgetown University center Patrick Ewing leapt above the rim and swatted it away. He was called for goaltending. That gave North Carolina two points. Ewing did the same thing the next three times down the court. North Carolina had scored eight points without putting a ball through the hoop. But Ewing had made his point. He was going to challenge every shot. North Carolina would have to work for every point.

That type of play was typical for Ewing. He was one of the most intimidating centers ever to play the game. He towered over opponents and rarely smiled on the court. Anyone who fought with him for a rebound risked getting a sharp elbow in the chest.

New York Knicks center Patrick Ewing gets ready to make a move against the New Jersey Nets during a 1994 game.

Ewing was so good in college that the NBA changed its draft rules for his arrival. In the past, the team with the worst record had the first pick. But the league did not want teams to lose on purpose so they could draft Ewing. So instead, all the teams that missed the playoffs went into a drawing for the first overall pick. That made Ewing the NBA's first lottery pick.

The New York Knicks landed Ewing. He never led the Knicks to an NBA title. But Ewing had a great career in the league's biggest market. After he retired, his No. 33 was retired by the Knicks. Ewing stayed in the NBA as an assistant coach, teaching the next generation of great centers.

10

The number of players in NBA history who scored at least 22,000 points and grabbed 10,000 rebounds in their careers when Patrick Ewing reached the milestone in 1999.

The New York Knicks' Patrick Ewing drives past Orlando Magic center Shaquille O'Neal during a 1996 game.

PATRICK EWING

Hometown: Kingston, Jamaica

College: Georgetown University

Height, Weight: 7 feet, 240 pounds

Birth Date: August 5, 1962

Teams: New York Knicks (1985–2000)
Seattle SuperSonics (2000–01)
Orlando Magic (2001–02)

All-Star Games: 11 (1986, 1988–97)

First-Team All-NBA: 1989–90

DAVID ROBINSON

David Robinson is proof that good things come to those who wait. Robinson was not a star basketball player in high school. He did not catch the eye of important college coaches. But he was a good student. So he decided to enroll at the US Naval Academy to study math.

Robinson then hit a growth spurt. He was 6-foot-4 when he started school at the Academy. By his sophomore year, he had grown seven inches. When he left the Academy he stood more than 7 feet tall. Robinson also had developed into the best basketball player in school history. He was a feared shot-blocker who had a good touch around the basket.

San Antonio Spurs center David Robinson shoots between a Phoenix Suns double team during a 1996 game.

The NBA wanted him. But Robinson knew his pro career would have to wait. All graduates of the Naval Academy make a commitment to their country. Robinson's commitment included two additional years serving in the Navy. After that, "The Admiral" was free to join the NBA.

71

The number of points David Robinson scored on April 24, 1994. The performance clinched the NBA scoring title that season.

The San Antonio Spurs picked Robinson first overall in the 1987 NBA Draft. The Spurs won 35 more games in Robinson's rookie season than they had the previous season. Robinson was named the NBA Rookie of the Year. It was just the beginning for him, though. Robinson later won Olympic gold in 1992 and 1996. He then helped lead the Spurs to NBA titles in 1999 and 2003.

Robinson showed his care for others by supporting many charities during his career. Because of this, the NBA named the plaque given to its community service award winner after him in 2003.

The San Antonio Spurs' David Robinson tries to work around Utah Jazz defender Karl Malone during a 1996 game.

DAVID ROBINSON

Hometown: Key West, Florida

College: United States Naval Academy

Height, Weight: 7 feet 1, 235 pounds

Birth Date: August 6, 1965

Team: San Antonio Spurs (1989–2003)

All-Star Games: 10 (1990–96, 1998, 2000–01)

MVP Award: 1994–95

First-Team All-NBA: 1990–91, 1991–92, 1994–95, 1995–96

All-Defensive Team: 1990–91, 1991–92, 1994–95, 1995–96

SHAQUILLE
O'NEAL

The word most often used to describe Shaquille O'Neal is "big." It described his body. It described his skills on the court. And it described his personality. O'Neal has always been larger than life. In fact, as a young teenager, his size fooled the man who would become his college coach.

It was 1985. Louisiana State University (LSU) coach Dale Brown was visiting US troops stationed in West Germany. O'Neal lived on the base with his mother and stepfather. His stepfather was a sergeant in the army. When Brown met the 6-foot-8 O'Neal, the coach asked him how long he had been in the service.

"I'm too young for the service, sir," O'Neal replied. "I'm only 13."

Los Angeles Lakers center Shaquille O'Neal dunks the ball against the Detroit Pistons during the 2004 NBA Finals.

O'Neal kept growing. Brown signed him to a scholarship. At LSU, he became known for his unique name and powerful dunks. O'Neal was then the first pick in the 1992 NBA Draft. And he quickly helped turn around the Orlando Magic.

Behind O'Neal, the Magic reached the NBA Finals in 1995. That was just the team's sixth year in the league. O'Neal then signed with the Los Angeles Lakers in 1996. He led them to three NBA titles in a row. He then won a fourth ring with the Miami Heat.

O'Neal's massive body and powerful post moves made him hard to stop close to the basket. He led the NBA in field goal percentage 10 times because he was such a strong dunker. During his career, he also acted in movies and recorded five rap albums. He achieved his life-long dream of becoming a reserve police officer as well.

52.7

The percentage of free throws Shaquille O'Neal made in his career—his game's one major flaw.

Shaquille O'Neal shows off the Los Angeles Lakers' 2001 NBA championship trophy, *left*, and his NBA Finals MVP trophy.

SHAQUILLE O'NEAL

Hometown: Newark, New Jersey

College: LSU

Height, Weight: 7 feet 1, 325 pounds

Birth Date: March 6, 1972

Teams: Orlando Magic (1992–96)
   Los Angeles Lakers (1996–2004)
   Miami Heat (2004–08)
   Phoenix Suns (2008–09)
   Cleveland Cavaliers (2009–10)
   Boston Celtics (2010–11)

All-Star Games: 15 (1993–98, 2000–07, 2009)

MVP Award: 1999–2000

First-Team All-NBA: 1997–98, 1999–2000, 2000–01, 2001–02, 2002–03, 2003–04, 2004–05, 2005–06

HONORABLE MENTIONS

Walt Bellamy – Bellamy finished in the top 10 in scoring and rebounding five straight years in the early 1960s. He played 14 seasons in the NBA, split mostly between the Baltimore Bullets, the New York Knicks, and the Atlanta Hawks.

Dave Cowens – Cowens won two NBA titles and a league MVP Award with the Boston Celtics in the 1970s. He is also one of four players—and the only center—ever to lead his team in points, rebounds, assists, blocks, and steals in the same season.

Dwight Howard – A four-time member of the NBA All-Defensive First Team through 2013, Howard won five league rebounding titles, four of them while with the Orlando Magic.

Dan Issel – Issel was the high-scoring star of the ABA's Kentucky Colonels in the early 1970s and later starred for the Denver Nuggets from 1975 to 1985.

Bob Lanier – Lanier was an eight-time All-Star who averaged 20 points and 10 rebounds per game throughout his 14-year career with the Detroit Pistons (1970 to 1980) and the Milwaukee Bucks (1980 to 1984).

Alonzo Mourning – An intimidating force throughout the 1990s, Mourning was a two-time Defensive Player of the Year and a seven-time All-Star, mostly with the Miami Heat.

Dikembe Mutombo – Mutombo was a feared shot-blocker who won four Defensive Player of the Year Awards and played 18 seasons (1991 to 2009) with six teams.

Bill Walton – Walton was one of the greatest college players ever at UCLA. He then led the Portland Trail Blazers to an NBA title in 1977 before his career was shortened by injuries.

GLOSSARY

assist
A pass that leads directly to a basket.

blocked shot
A play in which a shooter's field goal attempt is knocked down by a defender before it can reach the rim.

defense
The act of trying to stop your opponent from scoring a basket.

draft
A system in which leagues spread incoming talent throughout all of the teams.

goaltending
A violation that occurs when a defensive player blocks a shot that is on its way down or already on the rim, or when an offensive player touches a ball that is on the rim.

rebound
A missed shot that is caught by a player.

steal
A statistic awarded to a player who takes the ball away from an opponent or intercepts a pass intended for an opponent.

FOR MORE INFORMATION

Further Readings

Silverman, Drew. *The NBA Finals*. Minneapolis, MN: Abdo Publishing Co., 2013.

Silverman, Drew. *Basketball*. Minneapolis, MN: Abdo Publishing Co., 2012.

Websites

To learn more about NBA's Best Ever, visit **booklinks.abdopublishing.com**. These links are routinely monitored and updated to provide the most current information available.

INDEX

ABOUT THE AUTHOR

Patrick Donnelly is a veteran sportswriter who has covered the NBA, NFL, MLB, NHL, NASCAR, PGA, and college and prep sports for the Associated Press, MLB.com, and other websites and publications throughout the United States. He lives in Minneapolis, Minnesota, with his wife and two daughters.